TITB – Parking Lots

Increasing Innovation Through Parking Lots

Girish Maiya

This book is published as a reference guide for Innovators. Any reference to specific products or company is only to help out in product development process. The intention is not to promote or disregard any product or company.

For information contact; ugirishm@yahoo.com
Book and Cover design by Girish Maiya

Publisher: titbox.in

ISBN: 978-1522803935

First Edition: December 2015

Contents

This book is part of the 'Think Inside The Box' (TITB) series. Books in this series are all relating to innovation and the TITB concepts can be applied by individuals or at the corporate level. The first book explains a new concept called 'Think Inside The Box' which helps everyone to take up innovation in their own way based on their bandwidth, their knowledge and experience level and based on their own situation. Applying the same TITB concepts we have come up with one more innovative process, which is covered in this book.

This book introduces a new concept called 'Parking Lots' which can be used for bridging different processes or areas that have conflicts. This book also explains how 'Parking Lots' can be used for increasing innovation, either in your organization or in your personal life. Other important discussions that will help you to understand the concept easily, as well as a case study is included in this book.

This book would be helpful for anyone who wants to bridge two conflicting process, using parking lots or if they are seeing decrease in innovation level due to implementation of a specific process. Corporates can also use this book to bring in process improvements that can help to increase innovation in projects, departments, daily operations or organization wide. Parking lots are also helpful in integrating the innovations coming out of the R&D division into the main stream business of the company. Employee engagement and satisfaction can also be increased apart from customer satisfaction.

We would highly recommend that you read the first book of this series 'Think Inside The Box – Overview'. Even though the concept is explained briefly in this book and also explained as to how it can be combined with Parking Lots, understanding the full process of 'Think Inside The Box' will help you in developing an innovation mindset.

Apart from increasing innovations, parking lots can be used in other areas as well. A separate section is included in this book to provide some examples of such applications.

Conflicting Processes

You'll probably see many process, areas or approaches in your daily life and in your business or corporate life, that conflict in many ways. It need not be always completely opposite processes, but have some conflicting aspects like objectives or tasks or results etc. They might have similarities as well apart from the conflicts. The degree of similarities and conflicts might differ in each case depending on the situation. These conflicts might be visible not only in your personal life but also prevalent in complex organizations, communities, practices etc. Some of the examples of conflicting processes or approaches are; teaching kids how to save money versus making them happy; having a study job with decent income versus taking up once own interests; paying back good dividends to shareholders versus maintaining high employee satisfaction etc.

So, why are these conflicting processes or approaches important? Many times you'll be required to pick one process from these conflicting processes and sometimes you are required to balance between the two. Usually, you pick the one that you are comfortable with or commonly used ones and sometimes one of them might be forced upon you. By doing so you might be sacrificing some of the good things that can be achieved through the process or approach that you did not select. Hence, it is important to look at these processes, their conflicts and similarities. Lets look at how to fix this issue using parking lots, which is explained in this book. For now, you can look at all the processes and approaches you have picked either in your personal life or at your job and then identify all the conflicting ones that you have left out or tried to balance. Once we explain more about the concepts and processes relating to parking lots, we will discuss in detail about the process steps and how to implement them.

Parking Lots

We have been mentioning about parking lots many times till now, let us now try to understand the concept as well as the process. Providing parking lots is one approach that can help in bridging the gap between conflicting processes or areas. Its a solution where in a separate environment is created that is conducive to the process that was not selected but at the same time outputs are made compatible for integrating with the process you selected. This way you'll be able to benefit from good things in both the processes. Usually we refer to parking lot as a place to keep items that you cannot take up now but will take it up later when the situation arises. In this new concept we try to extend the functionality of the same parking lot to be a place which can process those items rather than just parking them in there, and also making those processed items suitable for easy and immediate usage.

Not clear? Let us try to put it in simple terms. When you have to pick between two conflicting processes but both have some good attributes that you would like to utilize, then instead of just picking one and rejecting the other, you pick one as the primary process and the other as secondary. Your main environment will follow the primary process but you will create an environment called parking lots which follow the secondary process. Then, you also alter the primary process to provide outlets into parking lot process and inlets to integrate outputs from parking lots back into the primary process. Apart from following the secondary process, parking lot process will also need some additional steps to make the output compatible with the primary process. Below is a simple diagrammatic representation of the approach, which could help you to visualize what was explained till now about parking lots.

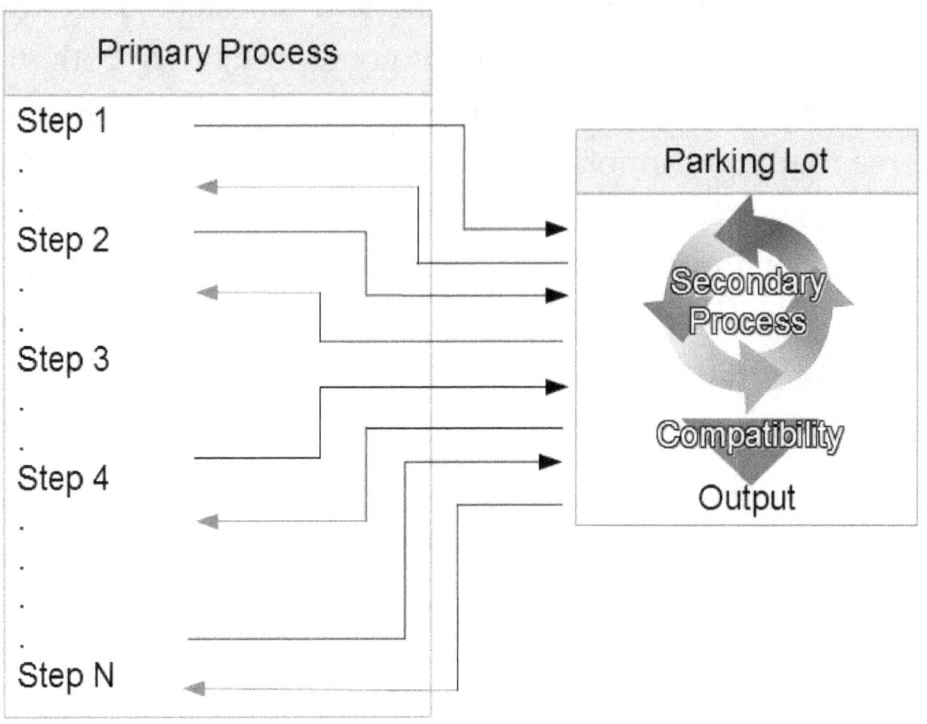

Still not clear? The case study section should help you in walking through a live example. However, let us try to illustrate it with a brief walk through for a quick understanding of the concept. Let us say there are two processes X and Y and they have conflicts. Your company wants everyone to follow process X but there are many good points in process Y that you would like to include in your project. So, you select process X for your project as that's what the company policy is, but you create a small area and assign some volunteers, which will be your parking lot. The parking lot will follow process Y. You pick some items in the project that does not fit well with process X and move them to parking lot. In the parking lot as process Y is followed, all the benefits of that process can be reaped. At the same time you follow some additional steps on these items so that they become compatible with process X. At regular intervals you provide options in process X to pick up items that come out of parking lot and then integrate it with your project.

So, through the implementation of parking lots you are able to bridge the gap between two conflicting processes or approaches. With the above explanations, diagrams and illustrations it should be pretty clear now about the parking lot concepts and processes. The case study section will make it further clear as to how you can implement the parking lot.

Innovation through parking lots

Till now we have discussed about parking lot process and how it can bridge gaps between conflicting processes. One of the major areas of usage of this process is to increase innovation involvement and output of an individual, project or a company. Let us now discus as to how this can be achieved.

Usually innovation requires a free environment where people can apply their mind without any restrictions, without pressure or micro management and try out different new things or new ways of doing things. There should not be any fear of failure as well. However, it is difficult to provide such an environment all the time in an organization as there are different stakeholders with different interests. As companies grow they tend to bring in more controlled processes which then hampers innovation and also tends to bring in other related problems. Having a free and uncontrolled environment becomes a nightmare for project managers as well. To overcome this issue, parking lots can be utilized.

The main environment will follow the more controlled process which will help the managers to easily manage the project. A parking lot will be created that has a free environment and with all the tools and resources required for innovation. The managers will identify items or areas that require innovation and then move it to parking lots. Based on the bandwidth and other requirements, resources will be assigned to parking lots to carry out innovation tasks in the free environment. Innovation outcomes are well documented and details provided as to how it can be used in the main process. The project managers review these innovations on a regular basis, pick relevant ones for integration with in the project. Through this way, managers will be able to have good control on the project while providing opportunity to increase innovation.

Below is the pictorial representation of how parking lots are used for increasing innovation:

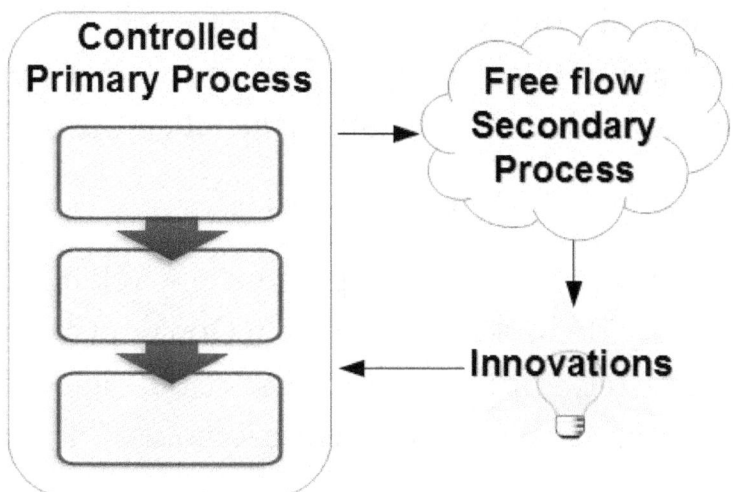

The items move from controlled primary process to parking lot process which has the free flow secondary process and the innovation coming out of them will then move back into the primary process.

How do I implement Parking Lots?

Now that you are comfortable with the concept of parking lots and understand how you can use it to increase innovation, let us look at some steps you need to follow for setting up the parking lots. You might have already followed a few steps by now based on the discussions in the earlier sections.

1. Identify processes:

    Identify various important processes or approaches that you are using. For now don't look at whether there are any conflicts or not, but just list down all the processes you are using. You can probably re-use policy and procedure documents for this as well, which usually lists out all the processes.

2. Identify conflicting processes:

Identify conflicting process in relation to the above identified processes. Don't just look for completely opposite processes, but look for any beneficial processes that were left out or not selected.

3. Analyze the conflicting processes:

Analyze as to which of these conflicting processes have some good things that you want to utilize. You can probably list out all the benefits, advantages, disadvantages etc. for each of the processes and then map it to the primary process, which can help you in analyzing the benefits etc.

4. Issues in current process:

Check if any issue or opportunity in the current process that could be overcome by the conflicting process. You can add issues and opportunities to the list you already prepared in the earlier step and then mapping it along with other items will help you in further analysis.

5. Finalize the parking lot process:

Finalize on which conflicting process or approach is a good candidate for implementing parking lot. The listing and mapping exercise performed in earlier steps should give you good data for making this decision. Sometimes you might have multiple processes as secondary process.

6. Setup parking lot environment:

Setup an environment for parking lot and assign resources based on the requirement. You can utilize an existing environment which is available or look at sharing environment across projects, which can reduce the cost of having a separate environment.

7. Alter the main process:

Alter the main process to include steps for identifying and moving items to parking lot. Brian storm with the team as to which of the steps in the primary process requires outlets to parking lot. You might add this to different steps in a phased manner to minimize the impact on the existing process.

8. Additional steps in parking lot:

Add steps in parking lot to make output compatible with the main process. Additional documentation, reviews, sign-offs, proof of concept, pilot implementation etc. might be required for making the outputs compatible with the primary process.

9. Start execution of the new process:

Start executing the altered process and items parking lot. First thing is to ensure good numbers of items are identified for parking lots. You might have to dig into earlier list of items to see if any items got rejected and could be used now due to the introduction of parking lots. It might need some hand holding as well, till the process stabilizes and team members get used to the new arrangement. Periodic trainings and awareness sessions might be required to remove any confusion due to having two environments and multiple processes.

The above are just some indicative steps. Based on your situation, you might have to skip some steps or add more. You can also follow a phased approach where in parking lots are initially small and take up only few important items, and then slowly you can expand it based on your experience. You might have to conduct some sessions with senior management to get their support and also to educate them about the benefits of parking lots.

Benefits

Let us look at some of the benefits of implementing parking lots, especially when it is done for increasing innovation. Understanding these will help you in ensuring your implementation is correct and you are able to reap these benefits.

1. Increased innovation: Obviously one of the main benefits is the increased innovation. Team members will be able to use the parking lots to try out new

ideas and bring the successful ones back to the main process. The good thing is, this can be achieved without loosing any control on the main process.

2. Multi-process benefits: While increase in innovation is one of the benefits, parking lots also help in reaping the benefits of multi-process and usually conflicting ones. You can identify benefits that are not available in the main process and then setup parking lots for making them available. This was probably unthinkable in the traditional approach.

3. Employee and customer satisfaction: Employees who are bored with the routine type of process followed by the main process, will be glad to get involved in parking lot and also to be a part of innovation. It could bring a complete culture change among the employees which in turn will increase their satisfaction. It could also attract good talents to the project as there will be opportunities to show case and improve their innovation skills. Bringing in innovation will also increase customer satisfaction as it could in turn improve efficiency and effectiveness as well as reduction in cost.

4. Better resource management: In most of the projects resource engagement is not uniform throughout the project life cycle. When the resource utilization is low in the main project, they can be deployed in the parking lots and get some innovation tasks completed. In the same lines if you have full time

resources in parking lots, you can deploy them in the main process when you have shortage of resources in main process. Parking lots also provide opportunities to re-skill and upgrade the resources based on the latest requirements.

5. Increased knowledge and experience: Team members involved in parking lots get to work on different items and hence they will have higher knowledge level and also experience. These knowledge and experience can then be used in main processes as well. Members who have worked in projects with parking lots will cultivate an innovation mindset.

These are just few indicative benefits of parking lots. Based on your situation and how it is implemented it could have many more benefits, especially small and indirect ones.

Advantages and disadvantages

Let us now look at some of the advantages and disadvantages of implementing parking lots in general and for innovation in particular. Understanding this will give you a comparative perspective of implementing parking lots. The main advantages are:

1. Freedom along with control: The main advantage of

implementing the parking lot is, you can provide some level of freedom in the parking lot process while you can maintain full control on the main process. While control is required by the project managers to ensure the project is going in good health, freedom is required for creative minds.

2. Flexible and collaborative: Since parking lots are secondary environment, you have the flexibility of expanding or shrinking it based on the situation. This flexibility will help in managing the resources better. You can also have it as a collaborative environment so that other teams from different projects can also contribute towards innovation. Collaboration will ensure that the benefits are utilized by large number of projects as well as ensure no duplication of effort.

3. Platform for phased implementation: Parking lots can also be used for implementing new things, like new processes, applications etc. If you are not very confident of releasing it in the primary environment, you can first release it in parking lot and based on the experience plan for release in the primary environment in a phased manner. It helps in discovering the unknown before going live, which in turn helps in better planning.

4. Theory to practice: Parking lots are useful to bring out all the theories relating to innovation to practice. It can also be used to try out project and other technology related theories to practice. While

separate R&D division can be used for innovation, you rarely get a place where you can do innovation as well as put it into practice simultaneously.

Some of the disadvantages are:

1. Additional cost of maintaining two environments: Even though there are long term benefits coming out of parking lots, in short term there will be additional cost of implementing and maintaining the parking lot environment and related resourcing. So, unless you are able to convince senior management about the long term benefits it is difficult to setup a dedicated secondary environment.

2. Used as short cut: Since the primary process is more controlled and parking lots are free flow environments, team members might use it as a short cut method, even though the items won't qualify for parking lots. If you don't have a good gate keeping process or oversight of parking lots, it could turn into a messy situation.

3. Difficult to monitor: As parking lots are secondary free flow environments, it is difficult to monitor the activities of resources assigned to parking lots. This might lead to inefficiency if not managed well. If the team members are not well motivated, non-project related works might creep into the secondary environments.

Again these are some high level advantages and

disadvantages and could be different for you based on your situation.

To make the parking lot process more clear, let us now go through a case study. John is a senior project manager in a software company. He is managing a project for a client, with the help of about 100 team members. As per the client's requirement the project is following water fall model to implement new functionalities in the application developed by the team. Even though the project is going smooth, John is seeing a decline in innovation and hence reduction in employee satisfaction as well. He is also not able to meet the high customer satisfaction requirement of his company. Competition is also increasing and hence John wants to show value additions in the project to the client. Hence, John is actively looking out for a way to solve these issues.

One of John's team mates had heard about 'Innovation Through Parking Lots' and has asked John if this could solve the issue. John has also invested some time to understand more about this new process and wants to use it for increasing innovation in his project. John has read through the materials on parking lots, understood the concepts and processes and then related it back to his situation. He has also come up with a plan for the same. Based on his understanding John has followed the below steps to implement parking lot, which is in the same lines as the steps provided in the earlier sections.

Think Inside The Box - Overview   19

1. Identify processes:

   The first step to be followed is to identify the processes that are used in the projects etc. It is pretty simple in John's case as the client's requirement for software development process is to follow the water fall model. So, John has identified that waterfall model is one of the causes for decrease in innovation. However, other models will not fit the client's environment as full control is required due to the nature of the industry and application functionality. As John is currently only looking at the project level scope, he has identified one process in SDLC. Later on he wants to increase the scope and look at other processes.

2. Identify conflicting processes:

   John has looked at other models that could probably lead to increase in innovation and agile and other iterative models are the best fit. He has discussed with other team members who have lots of new ideas to check which model fits well. Based on the brain storming agile methodology seems to be the best as it allows a lot of free flow and encourages innovation. Small sprints with quick innovation will also help John to show case it to his senior management and client to win their support.

3. Analyze the conflicting processes:

   Even though the feedback from team members is

to use agile method, John further did some analysis and found out that other iterative models might also help in unknown areas which require incremental innovation. So, John wants to keep the option open for using both the models. He is also open to bringing in any other models in the future based on the requirements.

4. Issues in current process:

John has already identified the main issue of decrease in innovation that can be resolved through parking lots. Also, currently the new features created by client R&D team are taking long time for customization due to following waterfall model. John thinks that using parking lots could reduce this time as well. Apart from this, talented resources are complaining about lack of challenges and scope for working on new ideas.

5. Finalize on the parking lot process:

Since both agile and iterative processes have their own benefits, John wants to include both in the parking lot process. However, since parking lot is supposed to be a free flow environment, the choice of which process to use has been left to the innovators. John is open to having any other processes in future if those could increase innovation.

6. Setup parking lot environment:

John has looked around to see if any old infrastructure is available for setup. After talking to different teams John is able to find an environment used as a sandbox by the R&D team. John is able to convince his managers to use the sandbox as the parking lot environment and installed all the required software and source code. Initially John does not want to spend too much money on this, till he is able to show some value addition. Later on, once he proves the importance of parking lots he wants to request additional budget for dedicated environment which he wants to implement across different projects of the client.

7. Alter the main process:

Below is the pictorial representation of a waterfall method, which is a highly controlled process.

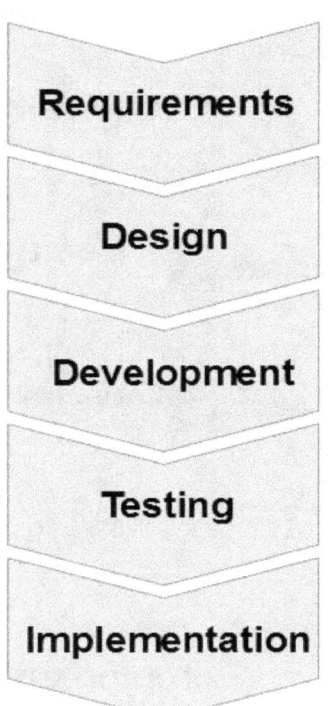

John does not want to alter the current process fully at once and would like to alter it in a phased manner, based on the initial experience. Since most of the innovation happens in design and development stage, he has provided two outlets from these two steps to the parking lots. Team mates are encouraged to come up with new ideas and if they don't fit into waterfall method John moves them into parking lots. Below is the pictorial representation of how the process looks after the alterations.

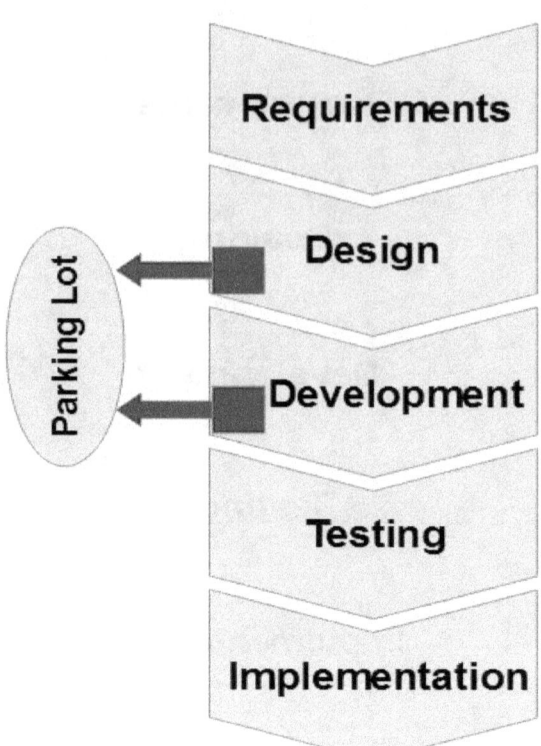

8. Additional steps in parking lot:

To make the output of parking lot acceptable for the primary process, John has added the following steps to the parking lot process. He is also in discussions with the client's team to understand if any additional steps are required as per their process requirements.

a) Get the output reviewed by an expert

b) Document the output along with details of implementation

c)   Perform a proof of concept in development or test environment and get a sign off from relevant stake holders

d) Include an appendix in the requirement document to make the output part of the primary process.

9.   Start execution of the new process:

John has gone through the items that were rejected earlier as they did not fit into the primary process and has put together a list of items that he would like to move to parking lots. He has also brainstormed with his team to come up with other items which could bring in innovation and moved them to parking lot as well. He has looked at the bandwidth of the team members and has come up with a plan for each item selected for parking lot. Buffers are also added to ensure minimal impact to the project.

Few items have already gone through the parking lot process and outputs have been brought back to the primary process. Below is the diagrammatic representation of the new process based on these executions.

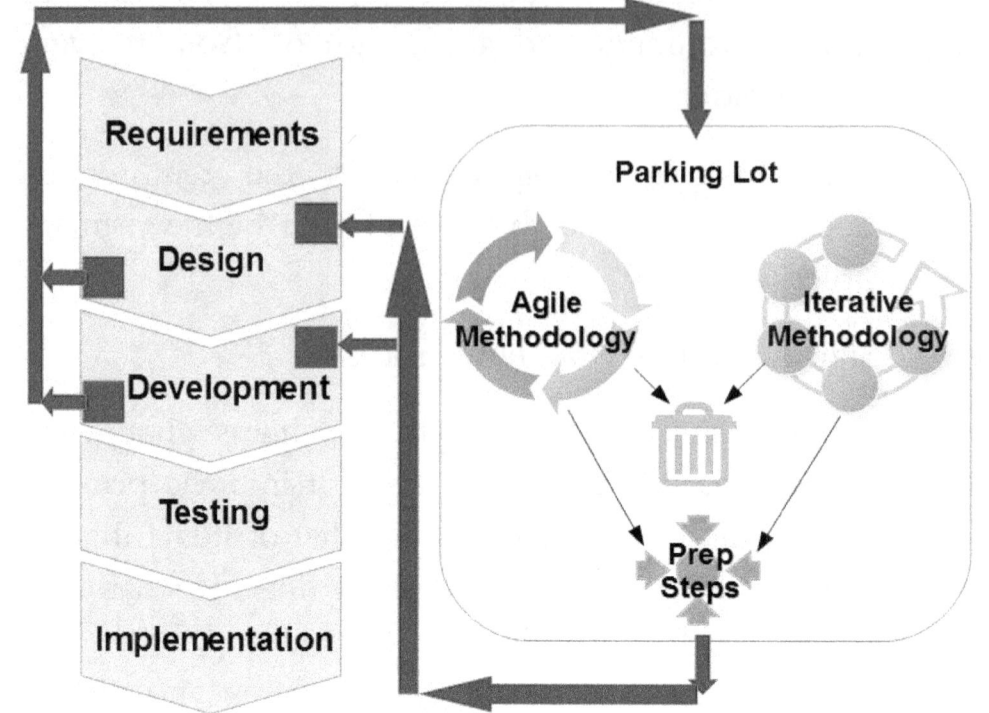

John is really happy with the outcome and is preparing to conduct sessions to senior management as well as clients to show case how he is able to increase innovation through parking lots. He has also started looking at the 'Think Inside The Box' concept and planning to implement it with in his team to further increase innovation by building innovation culture. These initiatives have not only increased the customer satisfaction but also employee satisfaction and hence the overall productivity of the project.

John has assigned few team members to document the process as well as to come up with a training program. Based on the experience till now they have come up with a process improvement plan as well. Client and senior management wants to increase the scope of parking lot and John has been promoted to the next level for his thought leadership.

As mentioned earlier parking lots help bridge the gap between conflicting process or approaches and hence it can be applied in different areas. We have already discussed in this book as to how it can used to increase innovation and its time now to explore other areas. Below are some of the examples in which parking lot process can be applied:

1. Family matters: You can use parking lots in family matters if there are conflicting processes or approaches. Matters that do not fit your principles or way of life but has benefits can be moved to a parking lot and slowly brought back after making it suitable. For example, your principles or way of life recommends you to save money and teach the same to your kids, which might be in conflict with making your kids happy. So, you can use parking lot to setup some boundaries to spend some money and make your kids happy, while you don't break your principles.

2. Culture building: Many times the policies and procedures of an organization come in the way of good culture building. There could also be different conflicting cultures that have benefits of their own.

Parking lots can be effectively used to bridge conflicting policies or procedures as well as conflicting cultures and then build a suitable culture in the company. For example, small groups of culture building teams can be formed to follow a parking lot process, who have exception to the company policy and procedures and then slowly bring those culture back into the main stream with minor modifications to the policy and procedures.

3. Community matters: In a community there are people from different beliefs, generations, professions etc. So, taking up community activities or decision making becomes difficult. Parking lots can be used to resolve this issue by moving conflicting activities to a parking lot. For example, small group of women can be formed to follow a parking lot process to take up women welfare and care, without breaking the beliefs or practices at the community level.

4. Bilateral issues: In a global economy, countries that have conflicts also need to work together, if they want to excel. The whole relationship itself cannot be stalled due to few conflicting issues. Parking lot would be a great way to move ahead with non-conflicting matters, while the conflicting matters are being worked out in parking lots.

There could be many more areas where parking lots can be implemented to resolve or bridge conflicting processes or approaches, especially where one is a controlled process and the other is a free flow process.

Think Inside The Box

'Think Inside The Box' is an innovation related concept that allows each and every one to contribute to innovation in their own way based on their own situation, experience, knowledge etc. Parking lot is an outcome of implementation of 'Think Inside The Box' concept and hence this book is included under the same series. Parking lots is a very good example to look at for the followers of 'Think Inside The Box' concept. Many more such useful topics are planned for the future under this series and hence it is suggested to regularly check TITBox.in for such publications.

At the same time since both the topics are relating to increasing innovation they can be used together to have a bigger impact on innovation efforts at your organization or personal life. Actually, they need to work hand in hand if you want to increase innovation in an organization. One is an **enabler** while other is an **executor**. 'Think Inside The Box' will enable in building innovation culture within the organization, while parking lots will establish an execution process to bring innovation to reality. Only having 'Think Inside The Box' process will not help as there is no good process to implement the ideas brought about by the team i.e. people are **enabled** but not able to **execute**. At the same time having only parking lots will not help as the team may not be able to come up with innovative ideas to implement i.e. **execution** process is in place but people are not **enabled**. So, both are complementary in nature and are required for increasing innovation.

Based on the above discussions it is better to implement both the processes in your organization. For further details on 'Think Inside The Box' please check the first book in the series named 'Think Inside The Box – Overview'. Depending on your situation, you can either implement both together or one after the other.

References

Below are the few references that will help in furthering your journey of innovation using 'Think Inside The Box' and 'Parking Lots'.

1. TITBox.in: We are planning to make titbox.in as a central repository for knowledge base on TITB concepts, projects, case studies, new ideas, collaboration, discussions etc. titbox.in will also work with TITB authors in helping them to publish articles and books. We are also planning on collaborative, crowd authoring of TITB articles. Keep checking the website regularly to get further updates on the 'Think Inside The Box' as well as 'Parking Lots' concepts and process.

2. Trainings and mentoring: titbox.in will also be setting up online as well as classroom based training sessions. These trainings will help TITB fans to

upgrade and update their skill-sets. Various formats of classroom trainings will be made available including practical workshops. Corporate entities and other organizations can select any of these trainings and titbox.in will make arrangements for sessions in the selected locations. Regular classroom sessions will also be scheduled in different locations which can be attended by anyone interested in TITB.

3. Useful materials: To promote TITB and help people to easily adapt and master TITB, many useful documents and other materials will be made available through titbox.in, which can be used by each and every one interested in TITB. Presentations and other materials will also be made available that will help TITB masters in promoting TITB within their organizations, communities or universities. Checklists and other reusable tools will be made available as well.

These are just few indicative examples of references. Also, since TITB and Parking lots are new, currently there are only few references available. But as these concepts and processes get matured, many more references will be available, including case studies and best practices. The contents will be updated accordingly as and when changes happen to the concept or the processes.

Girish Maiya is an author, innovator and entrepreneur. He has over 17 years of experience in various domains and companies. He has worked in the areas of financial and tax audits, ERP implementation and support, software development, testing, IT Audits, SOX audits, process review and improvements etc. He has worked in Indian as well as multinational companies and at various international locations. He has done consulting work for different companies in high tech as well as manufacturing industry.

His current passion is to innovate through open source hardware and also to publish books related to innovations. Girish has been practicing TITB approach for many years and now has given it a formal structure so that it can be used by others. Girish has already come up with many new ideas including the one given in the case study and would like to document the other ones for the benefit of TITB community. He is also interested in mentoring others on TITB concepts and implementation.

www.ingramcontent.com/pod-product-compliance
Lightning Source LLC
Chambersburg PA
CBHW071558170526
45166CB00004B/1711